T0353787

To The Littles

Discovering Self-Worth and Treasuring The Simple Things In Life.

CAMILIA ADAMS

This book is a work of non-fiction. Unless otherwise noted, the author and the publisher make no explicit guarantees as to the accuracy of the information contained in this book and in some cases, names of people and places have been altered to protect their privacy.

WestBow Press books may be ordered through booksellers or by contacting:

WestBow Press
A Division of Thomas Nelson & Zondervan
1663 Liberty Drive
Bloomington, IN 47403
www.westbowpress.com
844-714-3454

Because of the dynamic nature of the Internet, any web addresses or links contained in this book may have changed since publication and may no longer be valid. The views expressed in this work are solely those of the author and do not necessarily reflect the views of the publisher, and the publisher hereby disclaims any responsibility for them.

Any people depicted in stock imagery provided by Getty Images are models, and such images are being used for illustrative purposes only.
Certain stock imagery © Getty Images.

Interior Image Credit: Camilia G. Adams

ISBN: 979-8-3850-3052-1 (sc)
ISBN: 979-8-3850-3054-5 (hc)
ISBN: 979-8-3850-3053-8 (e)

Library of Congress Control Number: 2024915811

Print information available on the last page.

WestBow Press rev. date: 07/30/2024

WESTBOW
P R E S S®
A DIVISION OF THOMAS NELSON
& ZONDERVAN

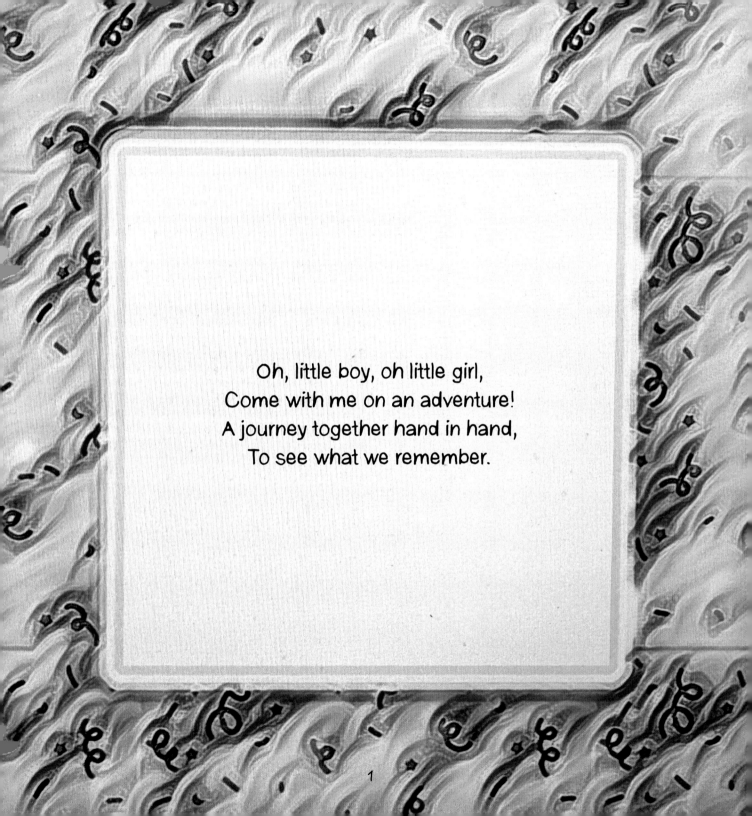

Oh, little boy, oh little girl,
Come with me on an adventure!
A journey together hand in hand,
To see what we remember.

It all began when you were born,
When you were born, oh littles.
You came as a marvelous gift from above,
Packaged and wrapped in God's sweet love.

Cooing and cuddling we held you so close,
You were simple perfection from head to toe.

3

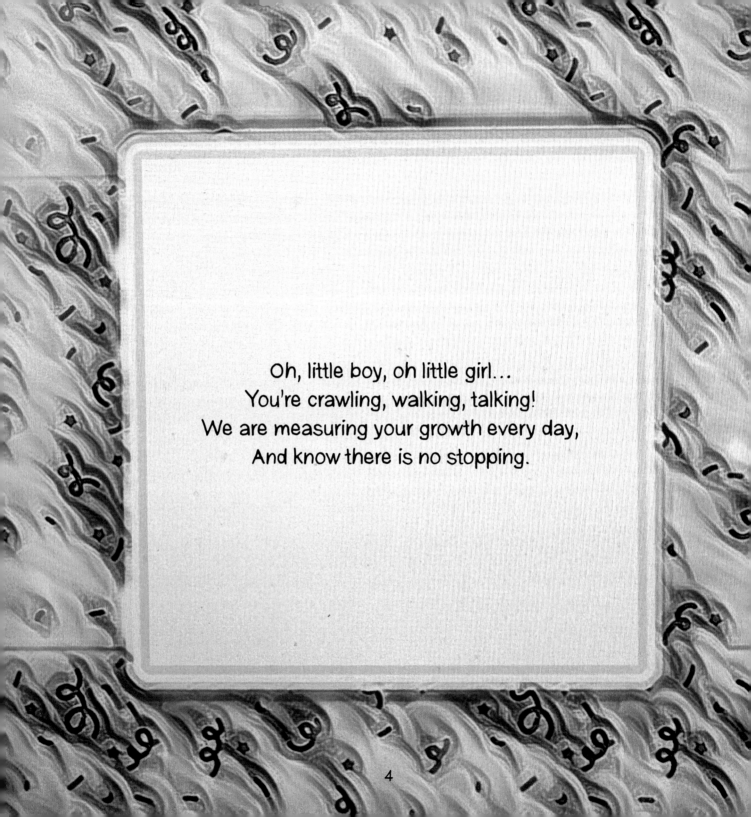

Oh, little boy, oh little girl...
You're crawling, walking, talking!
We are measuring your growth every day,
And know there is no stopping.

From "ones and twos" then tying shoes,
Each milestone brings emotion.
We can't help but smile with pride,
Our little is second to no one!

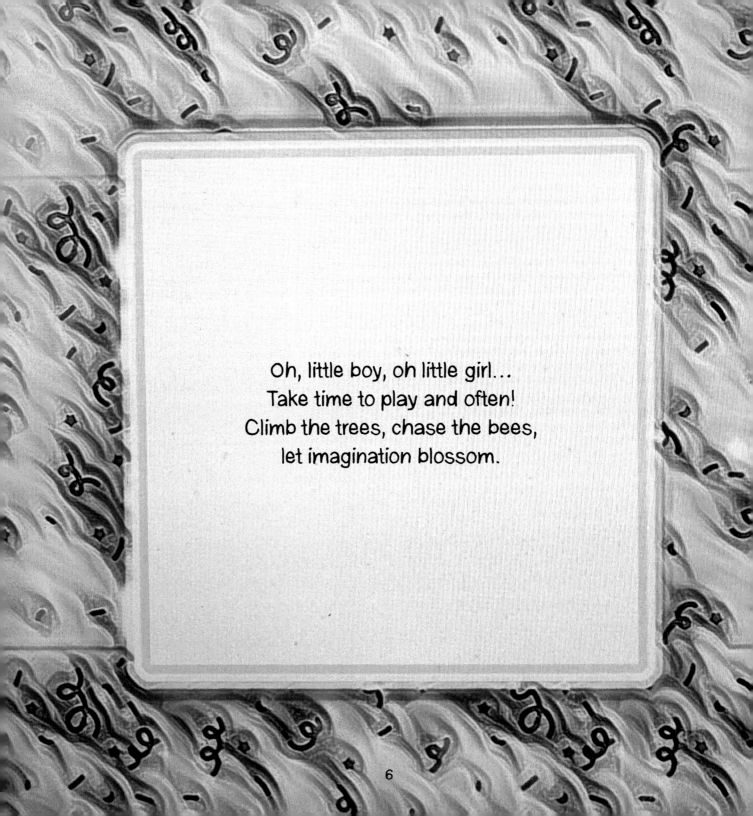

Oh, little boy, oh little girl…
Take time to play and often!
Climb the trees, chase the bees,
let imagination blossom.

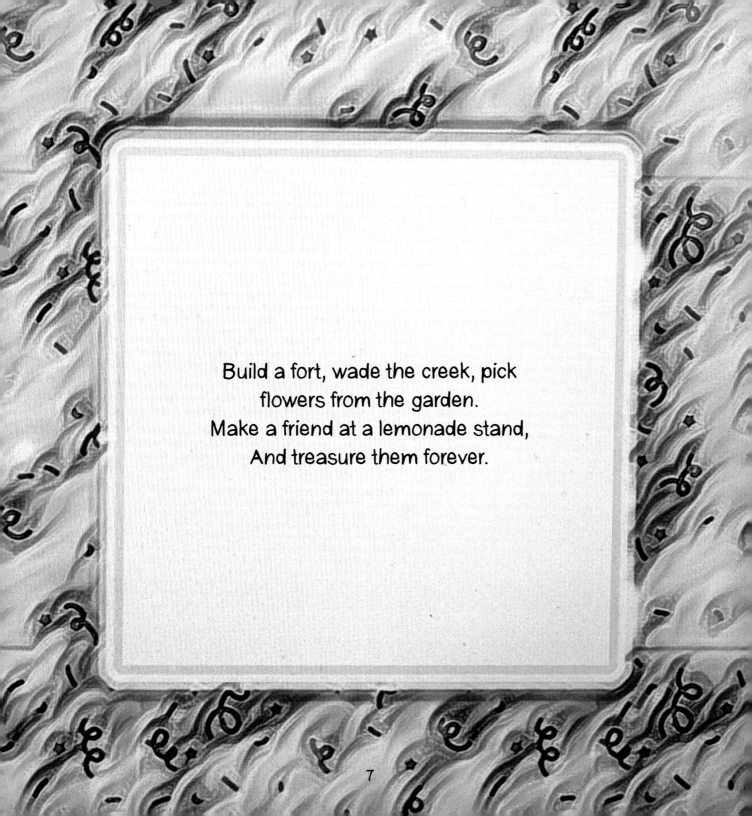

Build a fort, wade the creek, pick
flowers from the garden.
Make a friend at a lemonade stand,
And treasure them forever.

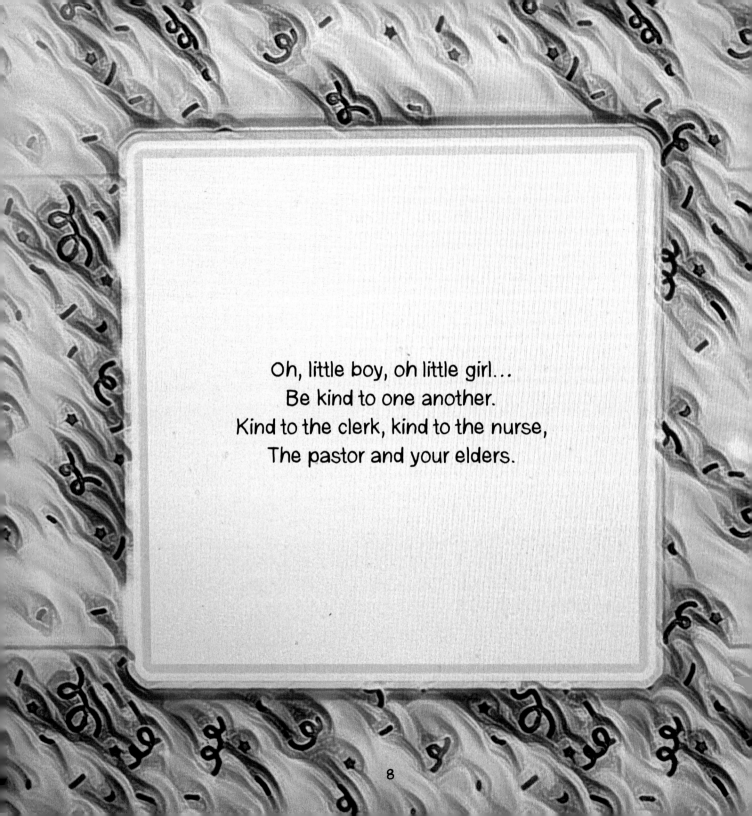

Oh, little boy, oh little girl…
Be kind to one another.
Kind to the clerk, kind to the nurse,
The pastor and your elders.

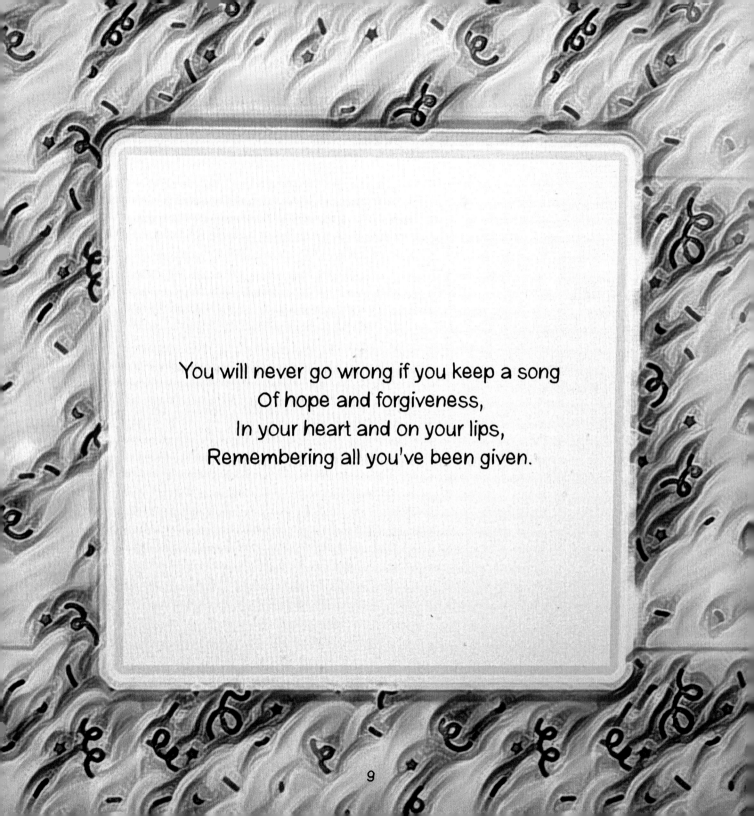

You will never go wrong if you keep a song
Of hope and forgiveness,
In your heart and on your lips,
Remembering all you've been given.

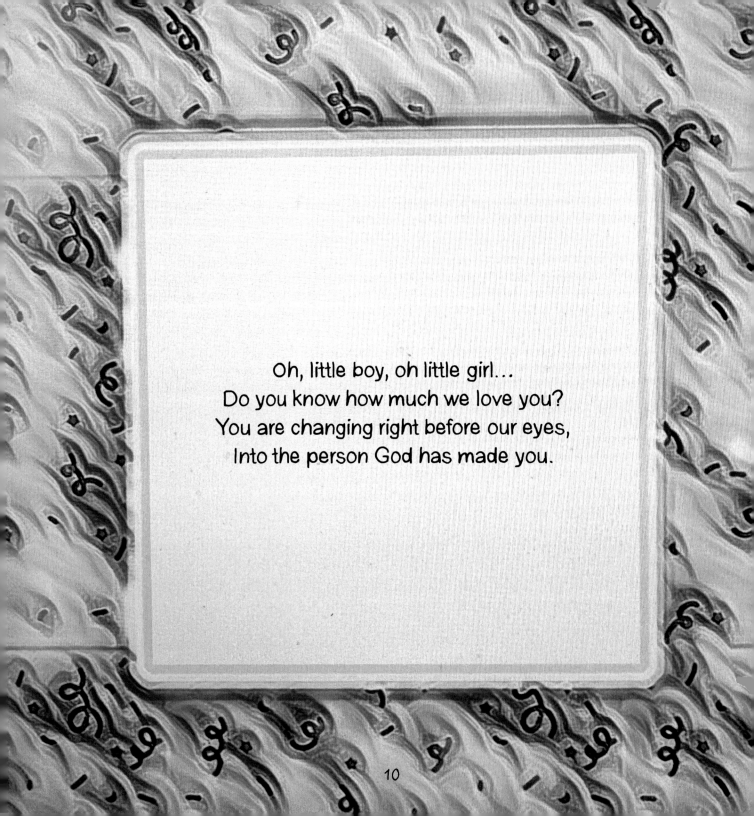

Oh, little boy, oh little girl...
Do you know how much we love you?
You are changing right before our eyes,
Into the person God has made you.

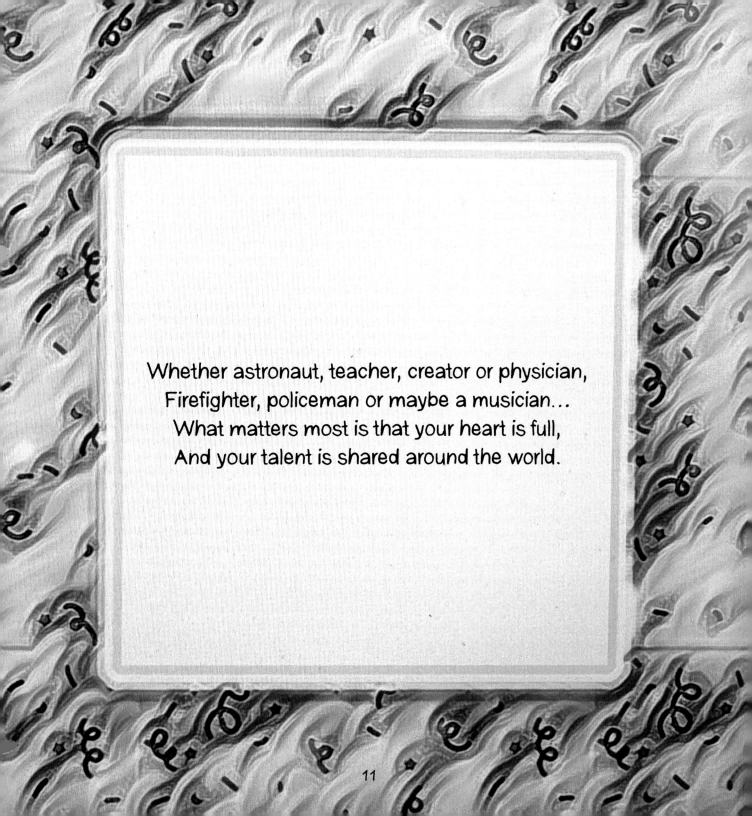

Whether astronaut, teacher, creator or physician,
Firefighter, policeman or maybe a musician...
What matters most is that your heart is full,
And your talent is shared around the world.

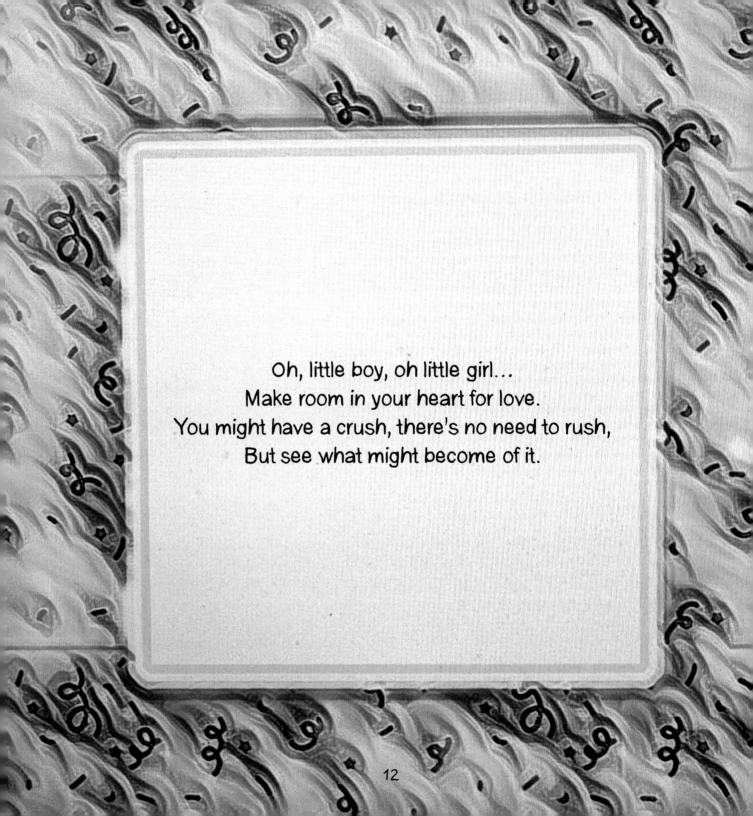

Oh, little boy, oh little girl…
Make room in your heart for love.
You might have a crush, there's no need to rush,
But see what might become of it.

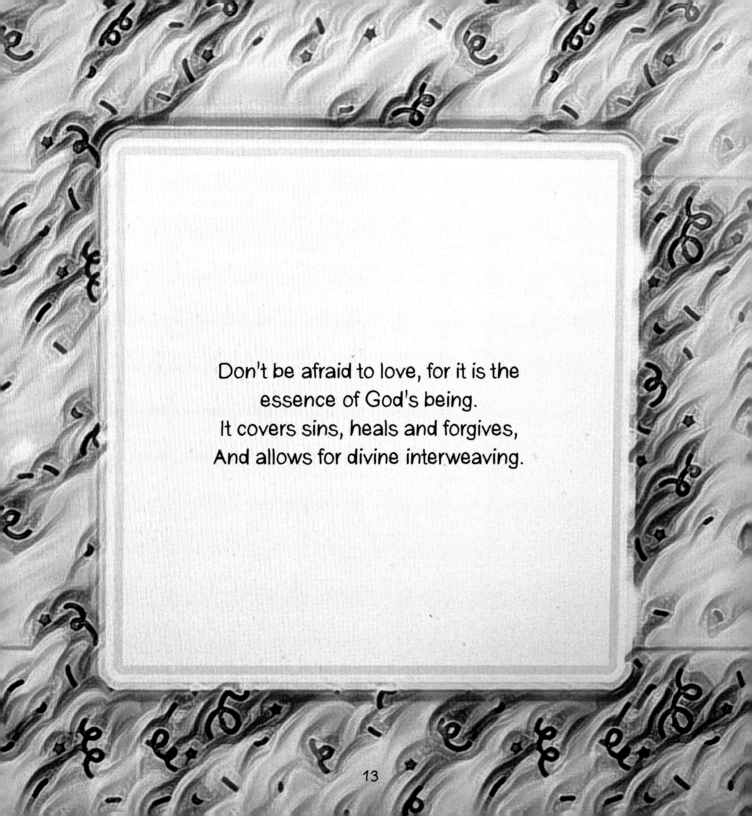

Don't be afraid to love, for it is the
essence of God's being.
It covers sins, heals and forgives,
And allows for divine interweaving.

Oh, little boy, oh little girl...
Being an adult isn't so easy.
You pay the bills, mow the grass,
Carpool the kids, pump the gas.

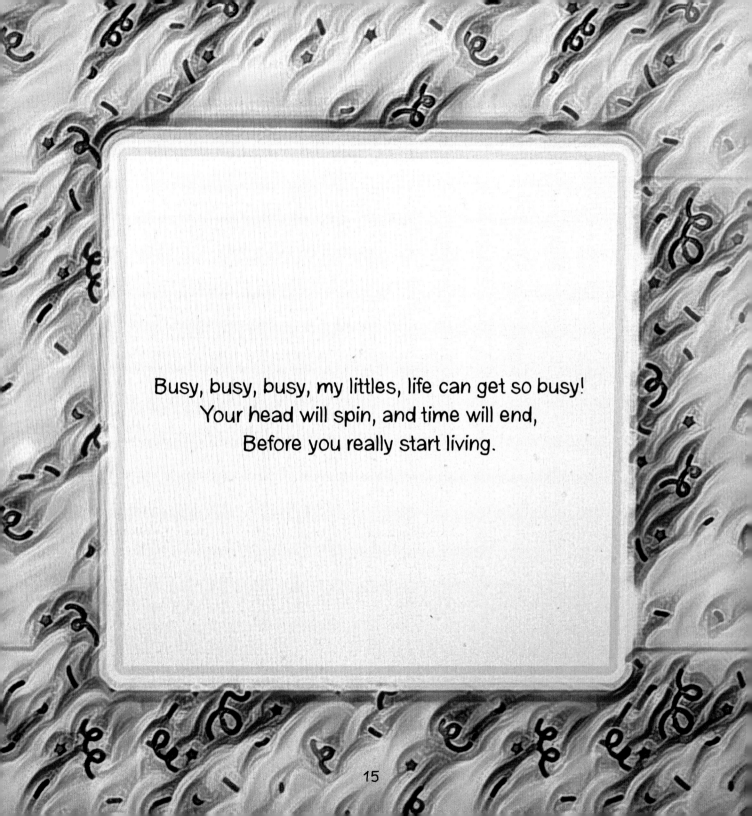

Busy, busy, busy, my littles, life can get so busy!
Your head will spin, and time will end,
Before you really start living.

Oh, little boy, oh little girl...
Love is so much stronger than hate!
Everyone is created equal,
And we all could use a clean slate.

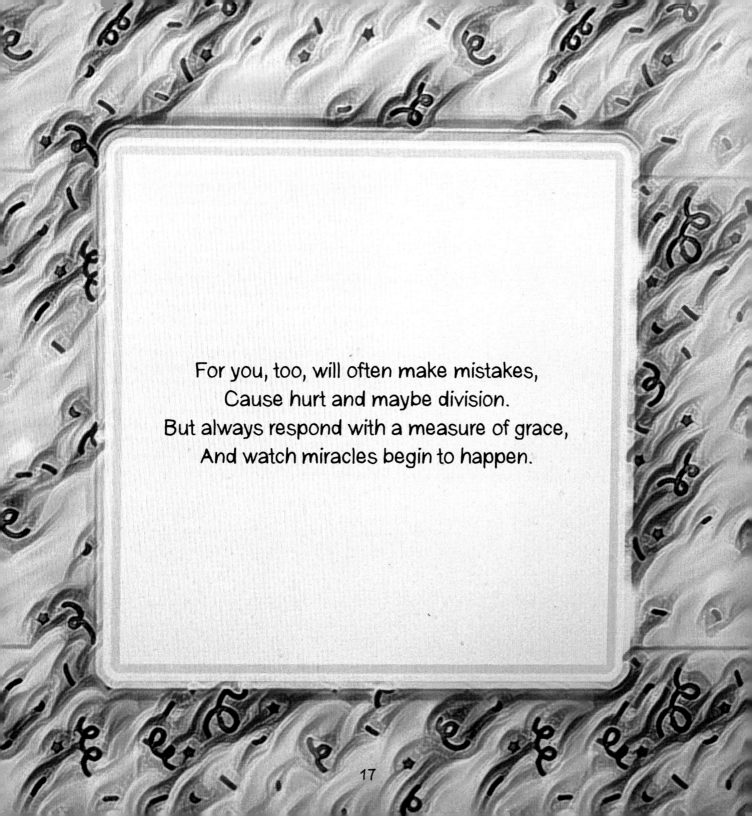

For you, too, will often make mistakes,
Cause hurt and maybe division.
But always respond with a measure of grace,
And watch miracles begin to happen.

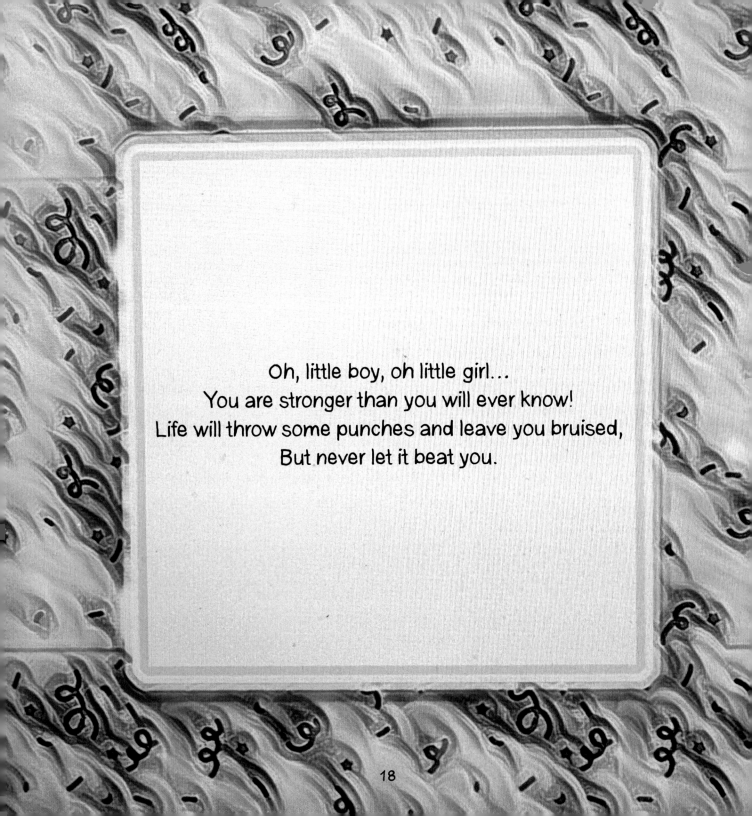

Oh, little boy, oh little girl...
You are stronger than you will ever know!
Life will throw some punches and leave you bruised,
But never let it beat you.

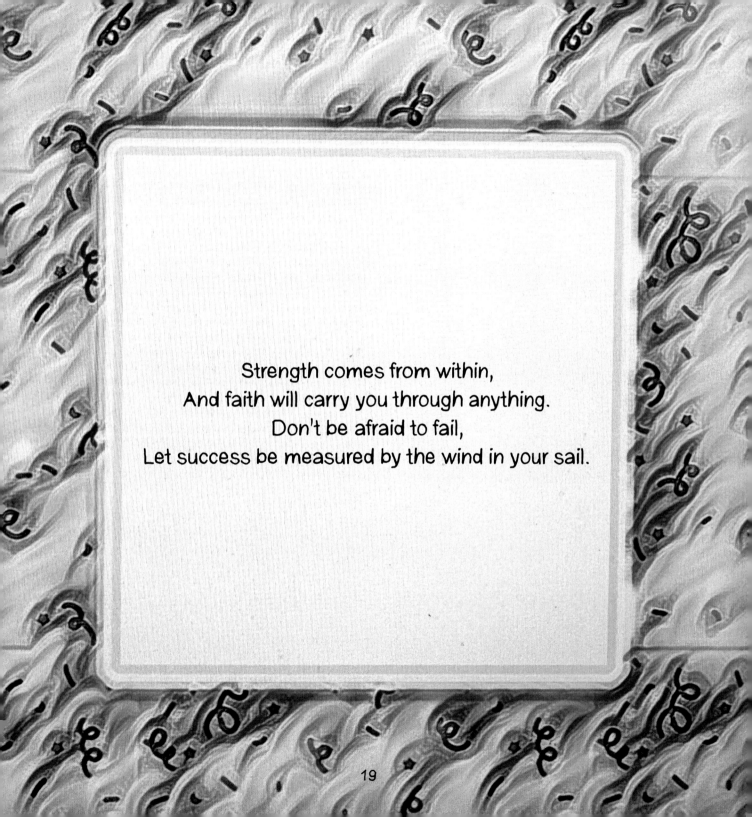

Strength comes from within,
And faith will carry you through anything.
Don't be afraid to fail,
Let success be measured by the wind in your sail.

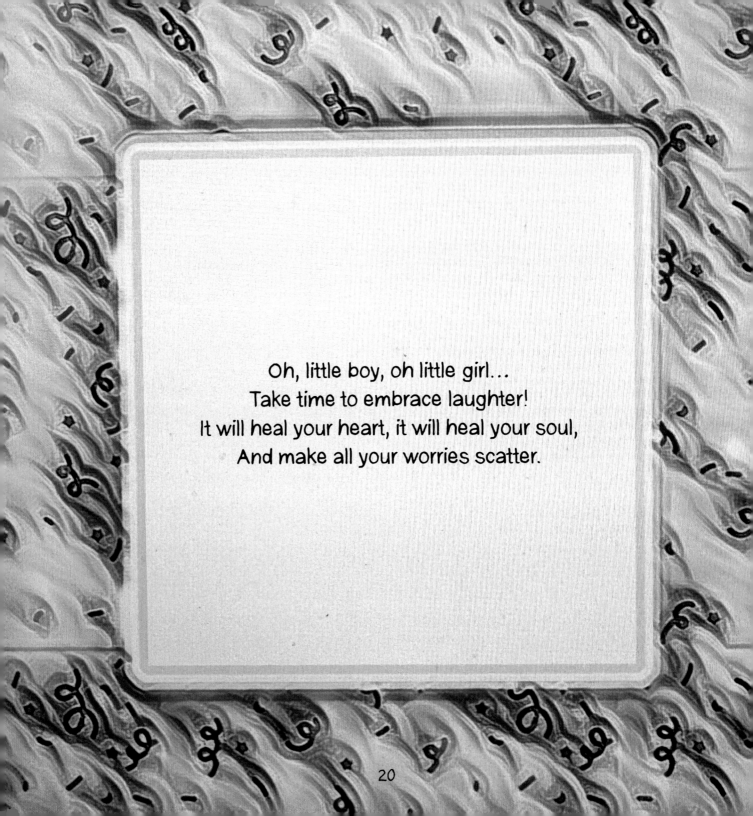

Oh, little boy, oh little girl…
Take time to embrace laughter!
It will heal your heart, it will heal your soul,
And make all your worries scatter.

Share a laugh with a friend, a laugh with a stranger.
Laugh at yourself in the face of danger.
Life is too short to not have fun,
No matter your age, you can still be young.

Oh, little boy, oh little girl...
Take time to stop and listen!
The rustle of the leaves, the birds in the trees,
And raindrops in the distance.

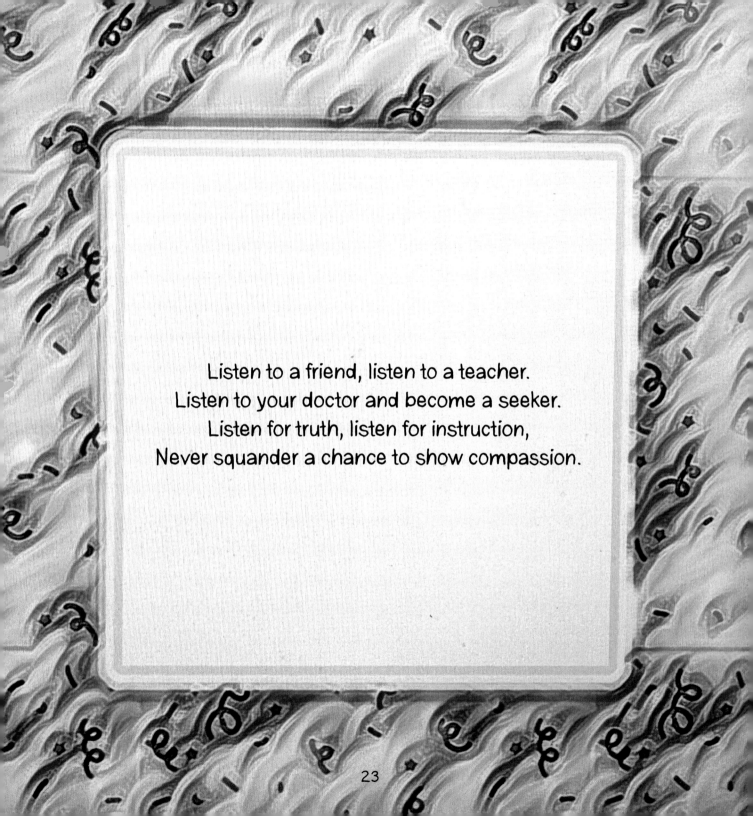

Listen to a friend, listen to a teacher.
Listen to your doctor and become a seeker.
Listen for truth, listen for instruction,
Never squander a chance to show compassion.

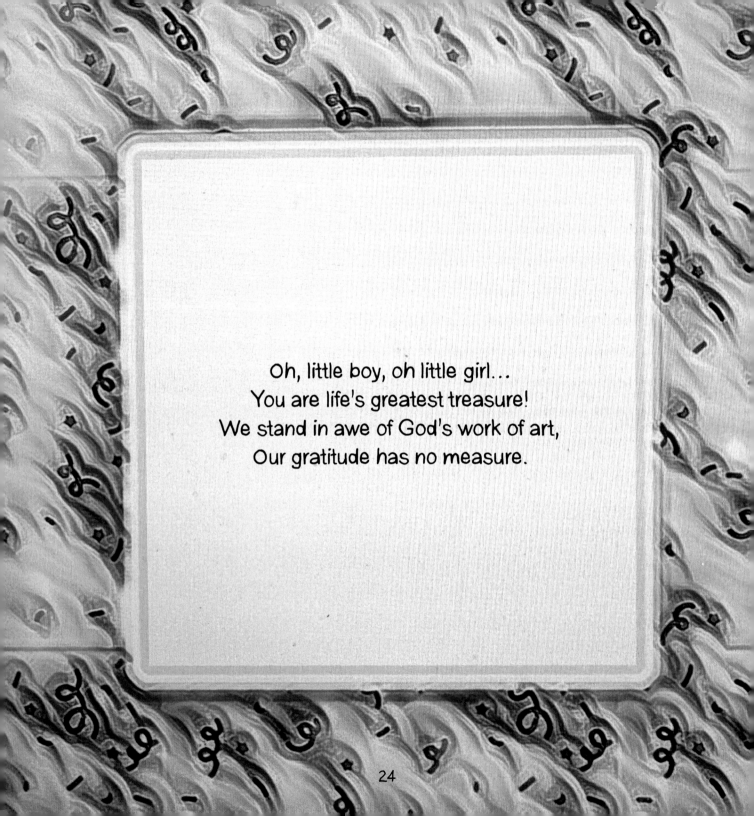

Oh, little boy, oh little girl…
You are life's greatest treasure!
We stand in awe of God's work of art,
Our gratitude has no measure.

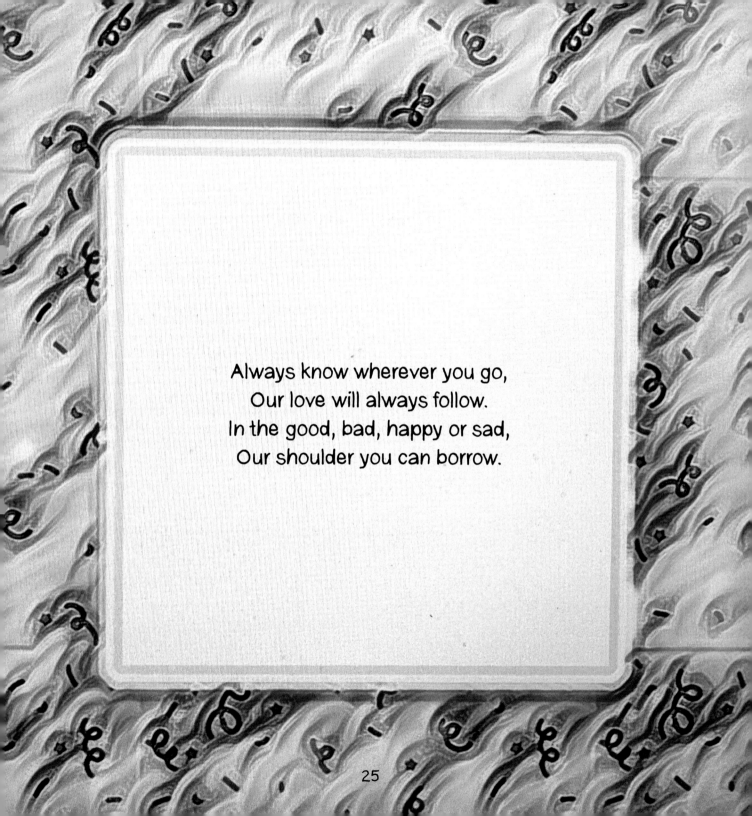

Always know wherever you go,
Our love will always follow.
In the good, bad, happy or sad,
Our shoulder you can borrow.

Oh, little boy, oh little girl...
At times you may need to cry.
Life has many ups and downs,
But all you can do is try.

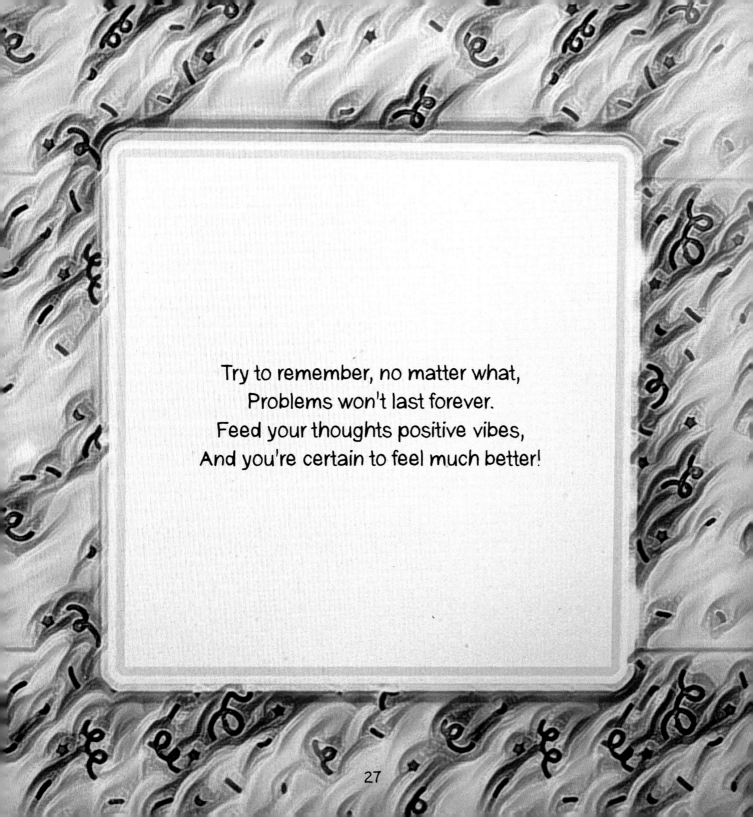

Try to remember, no matter what,
Problems won't last forever.
Feed your thoughts positive vibes,
And you're certain to feel much better!

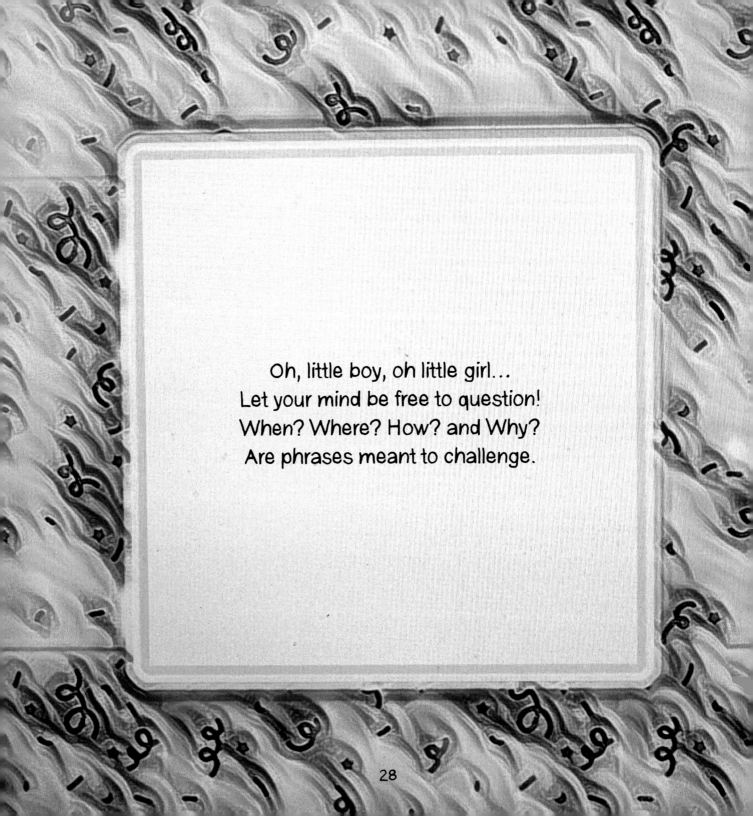

Oh, little boy, oh little girl...
Let your mind be free to question!
When? Where? How? and Why?
Are phrases meant to challenge.

Ask your grandpa, ask a vet
Gain knowledge from stories you'll never forget.
History will teach you what not to repeat,
It's up to you to take a lead.

Oh, little boy, oh little girl…
Don't forget to remember.
The simple things that brought you joy,
And peace on this adventure.

A hug, a smile, a laugh with a friend,
Words that heal, bring peace and forgive.
It's okay to embrace this life,
Just take it by the horns and enjoy the ride!

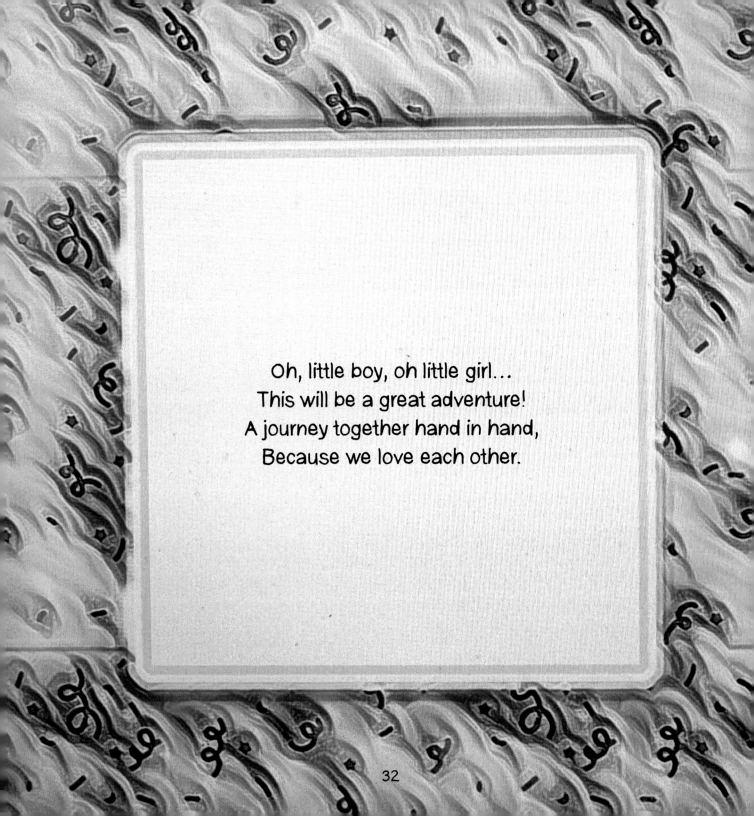

Oh, little boy, oh little girl...
This will be a great adventure!
A journey together hand in hand,
Because we love each other.

I hope that you will take the time,
To embrace these special moments in life.
Precious, precious, precious they are,
For you are the one that we live for!

Printed in the United States
by Baker & Taylor Publisher Services